FREEDOM NATIONAL—SLAVERY SECTIONAL

SPEECH

OF

HON. JOHN J. PERRY, OF MAINE,

ON THE

Comparative Nationality and Sectionalism of the Republican and Democratic Parties.

IN THE HOUSE OF REPRESENTATIVES, MAY 1, 1856,

In Committee of the Whole on the State of the Union.

Mr. PERRY. Mr. Chairman, in the discussions that have taken place upon this floor, and at various other places in the Union, the Republican party has been charged with "sectionalism." The authors of this groundless assumption have, in the same connection, boasted of the *nationality* of the Democratic party. These two propositions I now desire to discuss.

Prior to the meeting of the Thirty-third Congress, the country was enjoying a remarkable state of repose. The waves of agitation, which in former years had rolled over the country, had abated their fury, and ceased to disturb the peace or threaten the perpetuity of the Union. The discordant political elements had become quieted, and universal peace and almost unexampled prosperity reigned throughout the States. The people, a few months before, passed through a Presidential contest, and elected to the Executive chair of the nation a son of New England by an overwhelming majority.

General Pierce accepted the nomination upon a platform which declared—

> "The Democratic party will resist all attempts at renewing, in Congress or out of it, the agitation of the Slavery question, *under whatever shape or color* the attempt may be made."

The President, at the opening of Congress, declared, in the most emphatic terms, his determination to carry out the principles upon which he was elected. In his message he says:

> "But notwithstanding differences of opinion and sentiment, which then existed in relation to details and specific provisions, the acquiescence of distinguished citizens, whose devotion to the Union can never be doubted, has given renewed vigor to our institutions, and restored a sense of repose and security to the public mind throughout the Confederacy. That this repose is to suffer no shock during my official term, if I have power to avert it, those who placed me here may be assured."

The last Congress had been in session only a few months, before the country was startled with the unexpected rumor, that an old time-honored compact, which was originally entered into to avert the most threatening dangers, and which had been most religiously lived up to for more than thirty years, was to be ruthlessly abrogated. The sequel is too well known to need an extended notice. Leading men in the Democratic party, in utter violation of their past professions, forced into Congress the most *violent, fearful Slavery agitation* that ever distracted this country. President Pierce repudiated his pledges, trampled under foot the platform upon which he was elected, turned his back upon his friends that had elevated him to power, and used the whole force of his Administration to carry on this agitation, and expose the vast regions of Kansas and Nebraska to the inroads of African Slavery. The deed was done.

Slavery agitation, thus reopened in its most violent form, was not long confined to the Halls of Congress. It went out and spread all over the country, kindling up the raging fires of internal discord in every direction. The people became alarmed, and aroused themselves in their lion strength to meet the impending danger. Through all the free States they resolved that "forbearance had ceased to be a virtue," and that they would *resist* the outrage in the peaceable, constitutional way of settling such questions—at the ballot-box. This inaugurated a new political era. With a patriotism worthy of the men, and the cause which incited it, the freemen of the North laid aside their old party predilections, gave a paramount importance to the great issue forced upon them, and in almost every instance gave those members of Congress who had voted for the Kansas-Nebraska bill leave to stay at home. Only seven members from the free States, out of the whole number who voted for this measure, have found their way back to the present House. The repeal of the Missouri Compromise has completely broken down old party distinctions. The old Whig party, once mighty and powerful, and which in times past has had intellectual giants for its leaders, scarcely has a *name* in any State, North or South. The once glorious old Democratic party has been stabbed in the house of its friends; and, after retreating before the surging waves of popular indignation, can now only be found around the shades of the Presidential mansion, or in little squads about our custom-houses, post-offices, and such *other* places as are dispensed Executive favors, in the shape of "loaves and fishes." As a *national* party, it has no longer an existence. The causes, to which a brief allusion has been made, have created the *necessity* for another party. That party has been inaugurated; and as its principles are but the revival of the doctrines of the immortal Jefferson and the Republican fathers, it is perfectly natural and proper for it to assume the time-honored name of "*Republican.*"

As I announced in the commencement of these remarks, I shall now attempt to show that the Republican party is a *national* party; that it stands upon a platform of principles eminently *national;* and that no *national* man, North or South, East or West, can, with any show of consistency, refuse to stand upon it.

The Republican party, through its delegates at Pittsburgh, on the 22d of February last, adopted an address, containing a "declaration of its principles and purposes," which has been published to the world, and which is briefly summed up as follows:

"We declare, in the first place, our fixed and unaltered devotion to the Constitution of the United States—to the ends for which it was established, and to the means which it provided for their attainment. We accept the solemn protestation of the people of the United States, that they ordained it in order to form a more perfect Union, establish justice, insure domestic tranquillity, provide for the common defence, promote the general welfare, and secure the blessings of liberty to themselves and their posterity." We believe that the powers which it confers upon the Government of the United States are ample for the accomplishment of these objects; and that if these powers are exercised in the spirit of the Constitution itself, they cannot lead to any other result. We respect those great rights which the Constitution declares to be inviolable—freedom of speech and of the press, the free exercise of religious belief and the right of the people peaceably to assemble and to petition the Government for a redress of grievances. We would preserve these great safeguards of civil freedom, the *habeas corpus*, the right of trial by jury, and the right of personal liberty, unless deprived thereof for crime by due process of law. We declare our purpose to obey, in all things, the requirements of the Constitution, and of all laws enacted in pursuance thereof. We cherish a profound reverence for the wise and patriotic men by whom it was framed, and a lively sense of the blessings it has conferred upon our country and upon mankind throughout the world. In every crisis of difficulty and of danger we shall invoke its spirit and proclaim the supremacy of its authority.

"In the next place, we declare our ardent and unshaken attachment to this Union of American States which the Constitution created and has thus far preserved. We revere it as the purchase of the blood of our forefathers, as the condition of our national renown, and as the guardian and guarantee of that liberty which the Constitution was designed to secure. We will defend and protect it against all its enemies. We will recognise no geographical divisions, no local interests, no narrow or sectional prejudices, in our endeavors to preserve the union of these States against foreign aggression and domestic strife. What we claim for ourselves we claim for all. The rights, privileges, and liberties, which we demand as our inheritance, we concede as their inheritance to all the citizens of this Republic."

Now, let me candidly ask if there is anything *sectional* in the sentiments contained in the above declaration? If there is, then the whole country has been laboring under a delusion ever since our Government was formed. But, to be more specific, it is not to be denied that the great leading idea of the Republican party is the *non-extension of Slavery;* in other words, *opposition to its extension into free territory.* This is no *new* dogma. The heroes of the Revolution, the patriots of the early times, who shaped and fashioned our political institutions, entertained the same views, and incorporated them into their political action. They believed chattel Slavery to be a great moral, social, and political evil. So believing, they adopted every practicable mode in their power to *to prevent its spread;* at the same time looking forward to the day which should witness the fruition of their earnest hopes—its total abolition. To place this matter beyond all doubt or cavil, I will refer to a few well-authenticated historical facts, in proof of the position here assumed.

George Washington, in a letter to Robert Morris, dated Mount Vernon, April 12, 1786, said:

"I can only say that there is not a man living who wishes more sincerely than I do to see a plan adopted for the abolition of it, [Slavery;] but there is only one proper and effectual mode in which it can be accomplished, and that is by legislative authority; and this, so far as my suffrage will go, shall never be wanting."—*9 Sparks's Washington*, 158.

In a letter to John F. Mercer, September, 9, 1786, he expressed the same sentiment:

"I never mean, unless some particular circumstances should compel me to it, to possess another slave by purchase, it being among my first wishes to see some plan adopted by which Slavery in this country may be abolished by law."—*Ibid.*

And in a letter to St. John Sinclair he further said:

"There are in Pennsylvania laws for the gradual abolition of Slavery, which neither Virginia nor Maryland have at present, but which nothing is more certain than they must have, and at a period *not remote.*"

Thomas Jefferson, in an able article on the rights of the American Colonies, by him prepared and laid before the Virginia Convention which assembled in August, 1774, for the purpose of appointing delegates to the proposed Congress, remarks as follows:

"*The abolition of domestic Slavery* is the GREATEST OBJECT of desire in these Colonies, where it was unhappily introduced in their infant state. But, previous to the enfranchisement of the slaves, it is necessary to exclude further importations from Africa. Yet our repeated attempts to effect this by prohibitions, and by imposing duties which might amount to prohibition, have been hitherto defeated by his Majesty's negative; thus preferring the immediate advantage of a few African corsairs to the lasting interests of the American States, and the rights of human nature, deeply wounded by this infamous practice."—*American Archives, 4th Series, vol. 1 p.* 696.

Mr. Jefferson further declared his own sentiments in his Notes on Virginia, when he said:

"Nobody wishes more ardently than I to see an abolition not only of the trade, but of the condition of Slavery, and certainly nobody will be more willing to encounter any sacrifice for that object."

In the same work he further said:

"The whole commerce between master and slave is a continual exercise of the most unremitting despotism on the one part and degrading submission on the other. * * * * * "With what execration should the statesman be loaded, who, permitting one half of the citizens thus to trample on the rights of the other, transforms those into despots and these into enemies, *destroys the morals of the one part*, and the *amor patriæ* of the other! Can the liberties of a nation be thought secure, when we have removed their only firm basis, a conviction in the minds of the people that these liberties are the gift of God? That they are not violated but by his wrath? INDEED, I TREMBLE FOR MY COUNTRY WHEN I REFLECT GOD IS JUST, AND HIS JUSTICE CANNOT SLEEP FOREVER."

In the Convention which framed the Constitution, Mr. Madison declared he "thought it wrong to admit into the Constitution the *idea* that there could be property in man."—*Madison Papers*, 1429.

Gouverneur Morris said he "never would concur in upholding domestic Slavery; it was a nefarious institution; it was the curse of Heaven on the States where it prevailed." — 3 *Madison Papers*, 1263.

Mr. Gerry thought the Convention "had nothing to do with the conduct of the States as to slaves, but ought to be careful not to give any *sanction* to it."—3 *Madison Papers*, 1394.

Mr. Mason, of Virginia, said "Slavery discourages arts and manufactures. The poor despise labor when performed by slaves. They produce the most pernicious effects on manners. Every master of slaves is born a petty tyrant. They bring the judgment of Heaven on a country."—3 *Madison Papers*, 1391.

Mr. Ellsworth, of Connecticut, said "Slavery in time will not be a speck in our country."—3 *Madison Papers*, 1392.

Mr. Sherman, of Connecticut, said "he was opposed to a tax on slaves, because it implied they were *property*."—3 *Madison Papers*, 1396.

Mr. Williamson said "that both in practice and opinion he was against Slavery."—3 *Madison Papers*, 1428.

Similar views were expressed by other members. In the Conventions of the States, called to ratify the Constitution, similar opinions were expressed by the leading men in the same. I will only refer to a few of them.

James Wilson, of Pennsylvania, had been a leading member of the Convention; and in the ratification Convention of his State, when speaking of the clause relating to the power of Congress over the slave trade after twenty years, he said:

"I consider this clause as laying the foundation for banishing Slavery out of this country; and though the period is more distant than I could wish, it will produce the same kind, gradual change as was produced in Pennsylvania." * * * * "The *new* States which are to be formed will be under the *control* of Congress in this particular, and Slavery will never be introduced among them."—2 *Elliot's Debates*, 452.

In another place, speaking of this clause, he said:

"It presents us with the pleasing prospect that the rights of mankind will be acknowledged and established throughout the Union. If there was no other lovely feature in the Constitution but this one, it would diffuse a beauty over its whole countenance. Yet the lapse of a few years, and Congress will have power to exterminate Slavery from within our borders."—2 *Elliot's Debates*, 484.

In the ratification Convention of Massachusetts, General Heath said:

"The migration, or importation, &c., is confined to the States now existing only; new States cannot claim it. Congress, by their ordinance for creating new States, some time since declared that the new States shall be republican, and that there shall be no Slavery in them."—2 *Elliot's Debates*, 115

Nor were these views and anticipations confined to the free States. In the ratification Convention of Virginia, Mr. Johnson said:

"They tell us that they see a progressive danger of bringing about emancipation. The principle has begun since the Revolution. Let us do what we will, it will come round. Slavery has been the foundation of much of that impiety and dissipation which have been so much disseminated among our countrymen. If it were totally abolished, it would do much good."—3 *Elliot's Debates*, 6, 48.

But I will not consume further time to prove this point, but will only add an extract from a speech delivered by Mr. Leigh in the Convention of Virginia, in 1832, which fully corroborates the truth of this position. He said:

"I thought, till very lately, that it was known to every body, that during the Revolution, and for many years after, the abolition of Slavery was a favorite topic with many of our ablest statesmen, who entertained with respect all the schemes which wisdom or ingenuity could suggest for its accomplishment."

The founders of the Government not only left their testimony as individuals upon the question of Slavery, but their well-known opinions were incorporated into the Constitution and legislation of the country.

To go back to the Declaration of Independence, we find Washington, and Jefferson, and Franklin, and Sherman, and Pinckney, and their illustrious compatriots, solemnly subscribing their names to these "self-evident truths, that all men are created equal; that they are endowed by their Maker with inherent and inalienable rights; that among these are life, LIBERTY, and the pursuit of happiness."

The Constitution itself is a great chart of Liberty. Nowhere in it can be found the word "slave," or "slaves," so careful were its founders to give no implied sanction to the traffic in human beings. In its very commencement, in its preamble, it declares—

"The PEOPLE of the United States, in order to form a more perfect Union, establish justice," * * * "promote the general welfare, and *secure the blessings of liberty*," * * * "do ordain and establish this Constitution."

In the same instrument it is declared—

"*No person* shall be deprived of life, *liberty*, or property, without due process of law."—*Amendment, Art.* 5.

There is another provision contained in the Constitution, which for the last ten years has been the subject of warm discussion, both in and out of Congress. I mean that provision which gives Congress "power to dispose of, and make all needful rules and regulations respecting, the territory or other property belonging to the United States." In this connection, I do not propose to go into a discussion of the question, whether Congress has *constitutional* power to interdict Slavery in the Territories of the United States; but shall here content myself with showing how the framers of the Constitution understood it themselves.

On the 1st of March, 1784, Congress voted to accept of a cession from the State of Virginia of what was subsequently known as the Northwest Territory. On the same day, Mr. Jefferson, from a committee consisting of himself, Mr. Chase of Maryland, and Mr. Howell of Rhode Island, reported a plan for the Government. This plan embraced all the Western Territory, and all territory ceded or *to be ceded* by individual States to the United States. (See Journals of Congress, April 23, 1784.) One of the provisions of said plan is as follows:

"That after the year 1800 of the Christian era, there shall be neither Slavery nor involuntary servitude in any of the said States, otherwise than in the punishment of crimes whereof the party shall have been duly convicted to have been personally guilty."—4 *Jour. Cong. Confederation*, 371.

Territories were in this article of the Ordinance spoken of as States, because it was contemplated to erect the Territories into States. Under the Articles of Confederation, a majority of the thirteen States was necessary to an affirmative decision of any question. On the 19th of April a vote was taken on this proviso. The vote stood for the proviso—*six* States, viz: New Hampshire, Massachusetts, Rhode Island, Connecticut, New York, and Pennsylvania. Against it—three States, viz: Virginia, Maryland, and South Carolina. Delaware and Georgia were not represented. New Jersey, by Mr. Dick, voted ay; but her vote, only one delegate being present, could not be counted. North Carolina was divided—Mr. Williamson voting ay, and Mr. Speight no. From Virginia, Mr. Jefferson voted ay, and Messrs. Hardy and Mercer no. Of the twenty-three delegates present, *sixteen* voted for, and *seven* against—thus this proviso was defeated by a minority vote. The people were for it, and the States for it; but it failed by a provision which enabled the minority to control the majority.

In the same year, Mr. Rufus King, of Massachusetts, moved the proviso in the following form:

"That there shall be neither Slavery nor involuntary servitude in any of the States described in the resolves of Congress of the 23d of April, 1784, otherwise than in the punishment of crimes whereof the party shall have been personally guilty; and that this regulation shall be an article of compact, and remain a fundamental principle of the Constitutions between the thirteen original States, and such of the States described in the said resolve of the 23d of April, 1784."—4 *Jour. Cong. Confed.*, 481.

This was committed by a vote of two to one, and resulted in the celebrated Ordinance of 1787, which expressly *prohibited Slavery and involuntary servitude, except for crime, throughout the whole territory* [then belonging to the United States] FOREVER. This proviso received the votes of every delegate (with a single exception from New York) in the Convention. The First Congress under the Constitution ratified the Ordinance of 1787. In the Convention which framed the Constitution there were twenty men who were also members of the First Congress under the Federal Constitution. This proves very clearly that they understood that Congress *had* power, under the Constitution which they themselves had made, to prohibit Slavery in the Territories.

Thus history vindicates the fact, that the patriots of the Revolution, the members of the old State Confederation, the members of the Convention which framed the Constitution, and the members of the First Congress after the adoption of the Constitution, entertained the *same sentiments* upon the questions of Slavery extension and restriction that are now advocated by the Republican party.

But I will not stop here, but proceed to prove that the views of the Republican party on the constitutional right of Congress to prohibit Slavery in the Territories are sustained by the legislation of Congress from the meeting of the *First* Congress up to 1848, and that such legislation has received the sanction of every President, with a single exception, beginning with General Washington, up to, and including, President Polk. To maintain this proposition, I shall introduce *facts* direct from the records of the Government:

1. The Ordinance of 1787 was recognised by chapter one, first session of First Congress. There seems to have been no objection to it. Mr. Madison's name appears on the Journal of the proceedings the same day it passed. He was no doubt present, and concurred in the measure. The act was signed by General Washington.

2. On the 7th of April, 1798, an act was passed authorizing the establishment of a Government in Mississippi Territory. It authorized the President to establish therein a Government similar to that in the Territory northwest of the Ohio river, excepting the Jefferson proviso of 1787. It then *prohibited* the importation of slaves from any place without the limits of the United States. This act passed about ten years before Congress was authorized by the Constitution to prohibit bringing slaves into the States which were originally parties to the Federal compact. This act passed under the Administration of the elder Adams.

3. At the first session of the Sixth Congress, chapter forty-one, laws of 1800, an act was passed creating a Territorial Government for Indiana, out of the Northwest Territory—*reaffirming* the Ordinance of 1787—and was signed by President Adams.

4. On the 26th of March, 1804, an act was passed, dividing Louisiana into two Territories, and providing that all that part of the Territory south of the thirty-third parallel of latitude, now the southern boundary of Arkansas, should be erected into the Territory of Orleans. In this act there are three provisions in respect to Slavery in the Territory: 1. The importation from any place without the limits of the United States was prohibited; 2. The importation from any place within the United States, of slaves imported since the 1st of May, 1798, was prohibited; 3. The importation of slaves, except by a "citizen of the United States removing into said Territory for actual settlement, and being at the time of such removal *bona fide* owner of such slaves," was prohibited. This is one of the strongest cases on record to show the control of Congress over Slavery in the Territories. It was a direct prohibition of the domestic slave trade. This act was signed by President Jefferson.

5. On the 11th of January, 1805, an act was passed establishing the Territory of Michigan, *reaffirming* the Ordinance of 1787.

6. On the 3d of February, 1809, a similar Government was established for the Territory of Illinois, recognising the same Ordinance. These two last acts were under the Administration of Jefferson.

7. On the 4th of June, 1812, an act was passed

providing for the Government of the Territory of Missouri, and the laws and regulations in force in the District of Louisiana were continued in operation.

8. On the 3d of March, 1817, a Government was formed for the Territory of Alabama, and the laws then in force within it as a part of Mississippi were continued in operation. These acts were passed under Mr. Madison's Administration.

9. On the 9th of March, 1819, the Territory of Arkansas was formed from the Territory of Mississippi, and a Government established for it.

10. On the 6th of March, 1820, the inhabitants of Missouri were authorized to form a State Government, and Slavery prohibited in all that part of the Territory north of 36° 30′ north latitude.

11. On the 10th of March, 1822, a Territorial Government was established for Florida, containing provisions making it unlawful "to import or bring into the said Territory, from any place, without the limits of the United States," any slave or slaves. These three acts were signed by Mr. Monroe.

12. On the 20th of April, 1836, an act was passed establishing the Territorial Government of Wisconsin, *reaffirming* the Ordinance of 1787. This act was signed by General Jackson.

13. On the 12th of June, 1838, a Territorial Government for Iowa was established, extending the laws of the United States over the same, and signed by Mr. Van Buren.

14. On the 3d of March, 1848, an act was passed establishing the Territorial Government of Oregon, with the proviso forever prohibiting Slavery in the same. This act was signed by Mr. Polk.

Here is an almost uninterrupted series of legislative acts, commencing with the First Congress, and running through the long period of more than half a century, containing the official sanction of Washington, Adams, Jefferson, Madison, Monroe, Jackson, Van Buren, and Polk, directly recognising the constitutional right of Congress to *prohibit Slavery* in the Territories of the United States.

Thus the legislation of the General Government for more than half a century furnishes a precedent, in strict conformity with the platform of the Republican party, on the right of Congress to interdict Slavery in the national domain. If, then, the Republican party are to be denounced as *sectional*, on account of entertaining and defending these time-honored doctrines, then the revolutionary heroes were sectional—the signers of the Declaration of Independence were sectional—that immortal instrument was itself sectional—the framers of the Constitution were sectional, and so is the Constitution itself. Every President of the United States, from Washington to Polk, were sectional; and nearly all legislation of Congress, in the formation of Territories, for over fifty years, has been of the same sectional character.

Mr. Chairman, I now desire to call the attention of the Committee and the country to another leading idea in the Republican platform, to wit: *The* SUBSTANTIAL *restoration of the Missouri Compromise.* I have now no time to go into a historical detail of the circumstances that originally led to the adoption of this act of Congress in 1820; neither is it necessary; for the facts connected with the admission of Missouri into the Union are now pretty well understood. It is sufficient for my present purpose to remark, that, after one of the most stormy periods of excitement through which this country ever passed, it was solemnly agreed that Missouri should be admitted into the Union with a Constitution allowing Slavery; and that all territory which had been acquired by purchase from France, north of 36° 30′, should be *forever free.* The parties to this arrangement were the free States on the one side, and the slave States on the other. The prohibition north of 36° 30′ was both *absolute* and *perpetual.* I now propose to give some reasons why this contract should be restored in substance, if not in form.

1. Because the repeal of the Missouri Compromise was a breach of good faith. Each section of the Union had become a party to this contract. It became a matter of *national honor.* The North and the South had both agreed to it. Each party was not only bound by a solemn *act*, but there was an implied pledge of honor, incidentally connected *with* the act, of which the parties could not divest themselves.

2. The South received the consideration coming to them, *paid in hand.* The contract was ratified; and, with the ratification, Missouri was admitted. This repudiation is the more insulting to the North, from the fact that, just as soon as the consideration assigned her in this compact became of any value to her, she was cheated out of it. Good faith, fair play, and honest dealing all require the restoration of the contract.

3. This compact was abrogated under false pretences, and in its practical operation was a fraud upon the people. This will appear for two reasons:

First. At the time the Kansas-Nebraska bill was under consideration, it was declared over and over again, both in and out of Congress, that Slavery *never* would go into any part of these Territories. This pretext was used as an argument to quiet the excited feelings of the people, and reconcile them to the outrage. Charity would leave us to presume that no member of Congress would make such an assumption, and send it to the country, unless he believed it. If so, no greater mistake could have been made. In looking over the debates in the Senate upon the Nebraska bill, we find such opinions were expressed by Mr. Pettit, of Indiana; Mr. Hunter, of Virginia; Mr. Toucey, of Connecticut; Mr. Thomson, of New Jersey; Mr. Brodhead, of Pennsylvania; Mr. Badger, of North Carolina; Mr. Everett, of Massachusetts; Mr. Douglas, of Illinois; Mr. Dixon, of Kentucky; Mr. Jones, of Tennessee; and General Cass, of Michigan.

In the House, the advocates of the bill generally said the same thing. These declarations were sent all over the country, and had their effect. They were retailed out with great gusto by all the office-holders of the Administration, from the highest in grade and employment, to the four and six-penny postmasters and tide-waiters. The barrier of Freedom was stricken down; and what then became of all their pompous assumptions?

Slaveholders went into Kansas, carrying with them their slaves. The first Legislature elected under the organic law of the Territory, by slaveholders and "border ruffians"—a Legislature, the laws of which the friends of the Administration say are legal and binding—laws which the President has threatened to enforce at the mouth of the cannon and the point of the bayonet, enacted and placed upon the statute book of the Territory a law, declaring—

"If any person print, write, introduce into, or publish, or circulate, or cause to be brought into, printed, written, published, or circulated, or shall knowingly aid or assist in bringing into, printing, publishing, or circulating, within this Territory, any book, paper, pamphlet, magazine, handbill, or circular, containing any statements, arguments, opinion, sentiment, doctrine, advice, or innuendo, calculated to produce a disorderly, dangerous, or rebellious disaffection among the slaves of this Territory, or to induce such slaves to escape from the service of their masters, or to resist their authority, he shall be guilty of a felony, and be punished by imprisonment at hard labor for a term not less than five years."

Here is another section of this barbarous statute:

"If any free person, by speaking or writing, assert or maintain that persons have not the right to hold slaves in this Territory, or shall introduce into this Territory, print, publish, write, circulate, or cause to be introduced into this Territory, written, printed, published, or circulated, in this Territory, any book, paper, magazine, pamphlet, or circular, containing any denial of the right of persons to hold slaves in this Territory, such person shall be deemed guilty of felony, and punished by imprisonment at hard labor for a term not less than two years."

In the *Squatter Sovereign*, a newspaper published at Atchison, in Kansas Territory, by Stringfellow & Kelly, and which is receiving the patronage of President Pierce and his Administration, under date of February 19, 1856, I find the following advertisement:

"FOR SALE.—A very likely NEGRO GIRL, ten years old. Apply at this office. Feb. 18, 1856. 50 4w."

We prove here by one of the Administration organs—which, by the way, lauds Pierce and the Democratic party to the skies—that Slavery not only exists *de facto* in Kansas, but that little negro girls are publicly advertised and sold in that Territory.

I will give one more specimen of the barbarous code of the "border ruffian" Legislature, which is designed to corrupt the very fountains of justice, and establish and perpetuate Slavery in this Territory:

"No person, who is conscientiously opposed to holding slaves, or who does not admit the right to hold slaves in this Territory, shall sit as a juror on the trial of any prosecution for any violation of any of the sections of this act."

Thus facts prove that the argument that, on account of soil, climate, or other reason, Slavery would not go into Kansas in consequence of the repeal of the Missouri Compromise, was all a delusion; so far as it had an influence, it everywhere *deceived* and *cheated* the people.

Another reason, urged with great vehemence by the advocates of the Nebraska bill, in favor of the measure, was this: that it would "*establish the doctrine of popular sovereignty*," and give the people of the Territories the right to form and regulate their own domestic institutions. I have now no time to go into an extended argument to show the utter fallacy of this specious pretence, this false light, held out to blind, bewilder, and cheat the people into the support of a measure abhorrent to all their better feelings.

But I will call the attention of the Committee to one or two facts, which go to prove, beyond all controversy, that the friends of the bill, while they declared, when the same was under consideration, that the bill would confer upon the people of the Territories the right to legislate upon the question of Slavery in the same, *meant no such thing;* they were looking one way and rowing another; that while they were *pretending* to confer certain rights, they were forcing a bill through Congress, the very *object* of which was to deprive them of any such power.

Now to the proof. When the Kansas bill was under consideration in the House, an honorable member from Indiana [Mr. MACE] offered the following amendment:

"And the Legislature of said Territory is hereby clothed with full power, at any session thereof, to establish or prohibit Slavery."

This amendment was *rejected*—ayes 76, noes 94.—*Cong. Globe, vol.* 28, *part* 2, *p.* 1238.

Another amendment to said bill was offered by one of my honorable colleagues, [Mr. FULLER,] which reads as follows:

"And the Territorial Legislature shall have power to establish or exclude Slavery, as to them shall seem proper."

In offering this amendment, my honorable colleague said:

"This bill has been advocated at the North *solely* upon the ground that it gives the people of the Territory the right to legislate for themselves upon the subject of Slavery while in a Territorial state. I declare myself here to be the friend and advocate of that doctrine; and it is because this bill *does not establish* this great American principle, and vindicate this doctrine, that I am opposed to it in its present state. Now, sir, I wash my hands of any attempt to *deceive* them upon this vital point in the bill. My constituents shall not be *deceived* by me."—*Cong. Globe, vol.* 28, *part* 2, *p.* 1239.

My honorable colleague put the only reasonable, legal construction upon said bill that it would bear. This amendment, too, was voted down.

In further proof of the position I am now considering, I will cite the thirty-second section of the "act to organize Kansas and Nebraska." The phraseology of this section is peculiar. It was artfully drawn; and, while it *pretends* one thing, *means* quite another. It first undertakes to extend the "*Constitution*" over the Territory, by declaring that

"The *Constitution*, and all laws of the United States which are not locally inapplicable, shall have the same force and effect in said Territory of Kansas as elsewhere in the United States, excepting the act preparatory to the admission of Missouri into the Union."

Who ever before heard of such a monstrous absurdity? Congress, who derive all their power to act *from* the Constitution, here undertake to extend this great *fundamental* law of the land over a Territory within the jurisdiction of the United States. When did ever a Congress undertake before to *legislate the Constitution into a Territory?* Never, sir; never. No such provision was ever contained in any previous act organizing a Territory: hence, by fair reasoning, Oregon, Washington, Utah, New Mexico, and Minnesota, are all left without the protection of the Constitution; and Congress can have no jurisdiction over them, for the reason that that branch of the General Government derives all its *power to legislate* from the Constitution; and the only legitimate conclusion which follows is, that these Territories are each now so many *independent sovereignities*, owing allegiance to no power but themselves.

After declaring the Missouri Compromise "inoperative and void," the same section goes on to say:

"It being the true intent and meaning of this act, not to legislate Slavery into any Territory or State, or to exclude it therefrom, but to leave the people thereof perfectly free to form and regulate their domestic institutions in their own way, *subject only to the Constitution of the United States.*"

The deception lies in this—that, while this act professes to make a certain grant of power to the people of the Territories, it contains a *proviso* which, according to the Southern sectional construction given it by the Democratic party, *entirely takes it away.*

The argument to this: The Constitution is the great fundamental law of the United States.

To make the fraud less perceptible, by a sort of extra-judicial legislation, the Constitution is extended over the Territory. The grant of power here is made "*subject* to the Constitution," which is another piece of extra-judicial legislation. Then follow out the Southern construction—that the "*Constitution allows slaveholders to carry their slaves into the Territories, and there protects them in that kind of property,*" and you have the whole thing in a nutshell. Of course the people of a Territory cannot make a law *contravening* the Constitution. Thus it is plain that the act was *intended*, not to give "popular sovereignty," but to take it away; and, by a forced construction of the Constitution, *legislate Slavery into the Territory of Kansas.* In order to show that I am treating this matter fairly, and do not misrepresent our Democratic friends, I will read from remarks of an honorable member from Pennsylvania, [Mr. J. GLANCY JONES,] made in answer to certain interrogatories propounded to him by an honorable gentleman from Kentucky, [Mr. COX,] prior to the organization of the House. From the acknowledged talents and high standing of the honorable gentleman from Pennsylvania—from the fact that he was the author of the resolutions adopted by the first Democratic caucus of members of the House, and is a distinguished leader of that party—I feel justified in drawing the inference that he truly reflects the opinions of that party.

In answer to certain questions propounded by the gentleman from Kentucky, as to the legality of the Territorial laws of Kansas, he said:

"In my opinion, the Constitution *limits* the power of Congress to the extent of prohibiting them either from *establishing* or *abolishing* Slavery in the Territories. Admitting that view to be correct, I suppose it follows, as a matter of course, that the Constitution of the United States confers upon the people of the Territory no right to dispossess any man of his right to property, whether it be SLAVE or any other property. And, therefore, the Legislative Council of a Territory, though they may pass laws regulating the disposal and protection of property, have no right to so administer those laws as to establish or abolish the right to hold that property."

Another honorable member, ex-Governor Smith, of Virginia, in the same debate, said:

"If I had supposed there was any one opinion more universal than any other in the South, it was the opinion that a Territorial Government, while it remained in a state of infancy, has no power either to admit or to prohibit Slavery within its limits. I say that this Congress, this Government, having no right or power whatever to admit Slavery or prohibit it in the Territories, has no right or power to delegate that power to the Territories themselves."

A distinguished Senator from Mississippi, (ex-Governor Brown,) a few days since, in a speech in the Senate, said:

"It will be seen at once that the line of argument which I have marked out for myself will lead me to consider, to some extent, the doctrine of 'squatter sovereignty.' This doctrine, however well designed by its authors, has, in my judgment, been the fruitful source of half our troubles. Before the people of the two sections of the Union, having—as they supposed, though I think erroneously—hostile interests, and already inflamed by angry passions, were invited into the country, we, who gave them laws, should have defined clearly and distinctly what were to be their rights after they got there. Nothing should have been left to construction I believed, when the Kansas bill was passed, that it conferred on the inhabitants of the Territories, during their Territorial existence, *no right* to exclude, or in anywise to interfere with, Slavery." * *

"There seems to be a certain undefined idea in the minds of some men, that the sovereignty of a Territory is inherent in the people of a Territory; that it came to them from on high—a sort of political manna, descended from Heaven on these children of the forest. This doctrine, I confess, is a little too ethereal for me; I do not comprehend it; but this I know—if the sovereignty is in the people of the Territory, whether they obtained it from God or men, the conduct of this Government towards them is most extraordinary. It is nothing short of downright usurpation and despotism. We have now seven Governors appointed by the President, by and with the advice and consent of the Senate, to govern the seven Territories of the United States. We have seven different sets of Territorial Judges, appointed in the same way, to expound the laws for the seven Territories. We have Marshals to arrest, and District Attorneys to prosecute, the inhabitants of these *sovereignties*, in their own country. We require the Territories to legislate in obedience to our acts; and lest they may go astray, we sometimes oblige them to send up their laws for our approval. It has happened, time and time again, that their legislation has fallen under the disapprobation of Congress, and thereby become void What a *mockery* to disclaim the sovereignty yourselves, declare that it is in the people of the Territory, and then send a Governor to rule them, Judges to expound their laws, Marshals to arrest, and District Attorneys to prosecute them; and, finally, to require these sovereigns to send up their laws for your sanction; and then, by your disapproval, to render them null!"

The Richmond *Enquirer*, (Virginia,) a leading Democratic paper, recently contained an elaborate article, from which I make the following extract:

"We must, in the Cincinnati platform, *repudiate squatter sovereignty, and expressly assert State equality.* We must declare that it is the duty of the General Government to see that no invidious or injurious distinctions are made between the people or the property of different sections in the Territories. We do not mean to dictate. It may be that the assertion in the platform of the abstract proposition of State equality may suffice to carry along with it the consequences which we desire. But it is often charged that the Kansas-Nebraska bill contains the doctrine of squatter sovereignty, and that squatter sovereignty is the most efficient agent of Free-Soilism. Some [all] *Northern Democrats have maintained this ground.* Now, THIS GUN MUST BE SPIKED. It must appear from our platform that we maintain *practical* State equality, and repudiate that construction of the Kansas-Nebraska act which would defeat it."

The doctrine that the Constitution carries Slavery into the Territories, and there legalizes and protects it, and that the people of the Territories have no *right* under the Constitution to legislate upon the subject, except to "regulate" it, was, at the time of the passage of the Kansas-Nebraska bill, and now is, the doctrine of the friends of that measure.

Then I ask, sir, what becomes of your siren song of "*Squatter* Sovereignty," and the right given to the people of the Territories by the Nebraska bill "to form their own domestic institutions?" It is all a baseless humbug, an outrageous imposition, whose light only

"Leads to bewilder, and dazzles to blind."

There is one more very important reason why the Missouri Compromise should be restored. It is *to protect the people of Kansas in the enjoyment of their constitutional rights.* As we have already remarked, the Kansas-Nebraska bill was advocated on the ground that it would confer powers, rights, and privileges, upon the people of Kansas, not enjoyed by the people of other Territories under their organic acts. Now, what has been its practical operation? I have now no time to answer this question in detail. Instead of enjoying the extraordinary rights promised by the Kansas-Nebraska act, the people of that Territory have been hunted down like wild beasts—been waylaid and butchered in the streets; they have been lynched and mobbed; their houses sacked and burned to the ground; their printing presses thrown into the rivers; their property destroyed; and almost every indignity which the wickedness of men or devils could invent, showered down upon their devoted heads.

The Territory has been invaded by armed mobs, who have spread themselves into every settlement; the peaceful settlers have been forced to surrender their ballot-boxes at the point of the bayonet, and then driven from the polls. In order to show the kind of spirit which actuated these invaders, I read the following extract from the *Kickapoo Pioneer*, a paper which supports this Administration, and receives its patronage:

"The South must be up and doing; Kansas must and shall be a slave State Mark what we say, Southern freemen! Come along with your negroes, and plough up every inch of ground that is at this moment disgraced and defaced by an Abolition plough. Send the scoundrels back to whence they came, or send them to hell, it matters not which destination; suit your own convenience Sound the bugle of war over the length and breadth of the land, and leave not an Abolitionist in the Territory to relate their treacherous and contaminating deeds. Strike your piercing rifle-balls and your glittering steel to their black and poisonous hearts; let the war-cry never cease in Kansas again, until our Territory is divested of the last vestige of Abolitionism."

Sir, the "Constitution of the United States has been legislated into Kansas," and the people given "popular sovereignty;" and this is the kind of protection it has afforded them. All the protection the National Administration has afforded these hardy pioneers has been the protection the "wolf affords the lamb," by removing Governor Reeder, and sending out Wilson Shannon to enforce the bogus laws of a border-ruffian Legislature. There never will be any permanent peace in Kansas until the question of Freedom or Slavery is settled, either by the restoration of the Missouri Compromise, or her admission into the Union as a free State, which is substantially the same thing.

I now pause to inquire, Is there anything *sectional*, on the part of the Republican party, in their constitutional attempts to restore the national honor, and protect the people of Kansas in the peaceful enjoyment of their civil rights? If there is, make the most of it.

The second general proposition I now desire to discuss, is the "*Sectionality of the Democratic party.*" In pursuing this investigation, I intend to speak respectfully, but plainly. There are many reminiscences still lingering about the old Democratic party, of a pleasant character. It was once a great and powerful party. It was the party originally founded by Jefferson; and as we travel from its organization down the stream of time, we find in its front ranks some of the greatest and best men that ever honored and graced our country. It was once a party proudly standing upon a platform of national principles, around which the patriotic of every section, North and South, could consistently rally. But "how have the mighty fallen," and the "fine gold become dim!" Where stands the so-called Democratic party of the present day? Has it not changed fronts; abandoned its old landmarks; denied the faith, and gone over to sectionalism? These questions I now propose to discuss.

Slavery can in no just sense be termed a *national* institution. We have already shown that the founders of the Republic did not so consider it. Both the Constitution and the early legislation of the country clearly indicate the fact, that Washington, and Jefferson, and Madison, and their cotemporaries, looked forward to the ultimate extinction of this evil at an early day. The framers of the Constitution left Slavery where they found it—with the States—a municipal regulation, subject entirely to their jurisdiction and control. Being left to the States, it became of necessity *sectional.* Beyond the jurisdiction of the States where it exists, it has no legal protection. Again: Slavery is an *unnatural* right, and can only exist by virtue of the *local laws of the States.*

This question has been so decided by our judicial courts, North and South, over and over again. But in order to put this matter beyond all doubt, I will cite two or three authorities from the decisions of courts in *slave* States.

In the case of the State of Mississippi *vs.* Isaac Jones, the Court decided that

"The right of the master exists not by force of the law of nature, or of nations, but by virtue *only* of the *positive law of the State.*"—*Walker's Reports*, 86.

In another case in the same State, the Court say:

"Slavery is condemned by reason and the laws of nature. It exists, and can only exist, through municipal regulation."—*Hary vs. Decker, Walker's Reports*, 42.

The next authority which I read is from 2 Martin's Louisiana Reports, 402, 403:

"The relation of owner and slave is, in the States of this Union in which it has a legal existence, a *creature of municipal law.*"

I will cite one other authority to this point, out of the many that are found in the Reports. I read from the case of Rankin *vs.* Lydia, 2 Marshall's Kentucky Reports, in which the Court say:

"Slavery is sanctioned by the laws of this State. (Kentucky,) and the right to hold them under our *municipal* regulations is unquestionable. But we view this as a right existing by positive law of a *municipal character, without foundation in the law of nature, or the unwritten and common law.*"

Chattel Slavery has no existence except in one *section* of the country; therefore, any political party which favors Slavery, or in any way lends its influence to *spread* it, favors one section of the country at the expense of the other, and is most emphatically a *sectional* party. A party whose leading object is to favor the "peculiar institutions" of the *South*, can have no element of nationality about it.

I have already remarked that the Democratic party *was* once a national party. The leading men of the party, until within a few years, held that Congress *had* constitutional power to prohibit Slavery in the Territories, and that it is expedient to exercise this power. I have already spoken of the position of leading Democrats in the early history of the country. So well settled was this principle, that when the Wilmot proviso was first introduced into Congress in 1847, only two Democratic members from the free States voted against it. Among those who voted for it, were the Hon. Robert McClelland, now Secretary of the Interior; Senator Brodhead, of Pennsylvania; ex-Governor Dunlap, of Maine; and the late Senator Norris, of New Hampshire. The late lamented Silas Wright, General Dix, of New York, and other leading Democrats all over the country, favored the measure. The leading papers of the Democratic press came out for it. The *Eastern Argus*, the leading Democratic paper in Maine, and the New Hampshire *Patriot*, the leading Democratic paper in New Hampshire, both took strong ground for the proviso. More than this, a *majority* of the free States of the Union passed resolutions instructing their Senators in Congress to go for the measure, and in a majority of these States the *Democratic party* held the political control. In 1848, the following, among other Democratic members, voted for the bill organizing the Territory of Oregon, with a proviso forever prohibiting Slavery: Messrs. Allen, of Ohio; Benton, of Missouri; Bright and Breese, of Indiana; Douglas, of Illinois; Dodge, of Wisconsin; Dix and Dickinson, of New York; and Houston, of Texas.—*Congressional Globe.*

President Pierce himself, at a meeting held at Concord, New Hampshire, June 12, 1845, as reported in the New Hampshire *Patriot*, in reply to Senator Hale, said:

"He had only to say now, what he had always said, that he regarded Slavery as one of the greatest moral and social evils—a curse upon the whole country; and this he believed to be the sentiment of all men of all parties at the North. Mr. P. was free to admit that he had himself approached this subject of annexation [of Texas] with all his prejudices and prepossessions against it, and on one ground alone—its Slavery feature. His convictions on this subject were, as he had stated, strong—not the result of any new light, but deeply fixed and abiding. The only difficulty in his mind ever had been, that of a recognition, by any new act of our Government, of the institution of domestic Slavery; and he had found it extremely difficult to bring his mind to a condition impartially to weigh the argument for and against the measure."

In 1851, General Pierce, in the Convention of New Hampshire for revising the Constitution, left the chair, made a speech which was reported in the New Hampshire *Patriot*, and among other things said:

"I would take the ground of the non-extension of Slavery—that Slavery should not become stronger. But Congress have only re-enacted the old law of 1793. Union-loving men, desiring peace and loving their country, conceded that point—unwillingly conceded it—and, planting themselves upon this law against the outbursts of popular feeling, resisted the agitation which is assaulting all who stand up for their country. But the gentleman says that the law is obnoxious. What single thing is there connected with Slavery that is not obnoxious? Even the gentleman from Marlborough (Mr. Batchellar) cannot feel more deeply than I do on the subject."

New Hampshire and Maine have heretofore been the two leading Democratic States, not only in New England, but the Union. The Democratic party in these two States were the very last to falter, and the last to be conquered; for they, like General Taylor, never surrendered." As long ago as 1828, the county of Cumberland, in Maine, the larger portion of which is in my district, "solitary and alone" *in all New England, gave her electoral vote to Andrew Jackson.* For this act of fidelity to the gallant old hero, this county was long known as the "Star in the East;" and the now venerable James C. Churchill, who was the standard-bearer of the "unterrified" in that great fight, is now an honored member of the Republican party. I have seen a letter written by him, dated Portland, March 21, 1856, in answer to an invitation from the "American Republicans" of Dover, New Hampshire, to meet with them and celebrate the late glorious victory in that State, in which he says:

"I congratulate you most heartily and sincerely in having obtained a victory so signal and so glorious. It seems to me the advocate of 'Rum' lacks good morals and good judgment; the advocate of extension of 'Slavery' lacks good sense and good principles, and every good thing for which our fathers fought and conquered in the Revolution."

In 1832, Maine gave her ten electoral votes to Old Hickory, and gallant New Hampshire wheeled in by her side, with her seven. In 1836, they both went for Van Buren. In 1840, the Democracy of Maine, after a terrible fight, was beaten only by a few hundreds. "Hard cider, log cabins, and gold spoons," were too much for her. But New Hampshire, firm as her "granite hills," breasted the storm, withstood the shock, and gave her seven electoral votes for Van Buren. In 1844, both States went for James K. Polk; in 1848, both voted for General Cass; and in 1852, both, by overwhelming majorities, chose electors for Franklin Pierce.

With this clean Democratic record, where has the Democratic party in these States stood upon the question of Slavery prohibition in the Territories? I answer, just where the Republican party now stand; and I will proceed to prove it.

The Democratic State Committee of New Hampshire, in October, 1847, passed the following resolution:

"*Resolved*, That we declare it OUR SOLEMN CONVICTION, as the Democratic party have heretofore done, that neither *Slavery nor involuntary servitude* should hereafter exist in any Territory which may be acquired by or annexed to the United States; and that we approve of the votes of our delegation in Congress in favor of the Wilmot Proviso."

In 1848, the Legislature of that State, which had an overwhelming Democratic majority, resolved as follows:

"*Resolved by the Senate and House of Representatives in General Court convened*, That we are in favor of the passage of a law, by Congress, *forever prohibiting Slavery* in New Mexico and California, *and in all other Territories* now acquired, or hereafter to be acquired, by the United States, in which Slavery does not exist at the time of such acquisition."

And in 1849, the New Hampshire Legislature, still strongly Democratic, unanimously adopted the following resolutions:

"*Resolved by the Senate and House of Representatives in General Court convened*, That, opposed to every form of oppression, the people of New Hampshire have ever viewed with deep regret the existence of Slavery in this Union; that while they have steadfastly supported all sections in their constitutional rights, they have not only lamented its existence as a great social evil, but regarded it as *fraught with danger to the peace and welfare of the nation.*

"*Resolved*, That while we respect the rights of the slaveholding as well as the free portions of this Union—while we will not willingly consent that wrong be done to any member of the glorious Confederacy to which we belong, we are *firmly and unalterably opposed to the extension of Slavery over any portion of American soil now free.*

"*Resolved*, That, in our opinion, Congress has the *constitutional power to abolish the slave trade and Slavery in the District of Columbia;* and that our Senators *be instructed*, and our Representatives *be requested, to take all constitutional measures* to accomplish these objects.—*See Speech of Senator Hale.*

But how have the Democratic "veterans of an hundred battles" in Maine stood upon this question? We will see.

In 1847, Hon. John W. Dana was Governor of Maine, and the Legislature was strongly Democratic. In his annual message, Governor Dana said:

"The territory which we may acquire as indemnity for claims upon Mexico is free; shall it be made slave territory? The sentiment of the free States is profound, sincere, and almost universal, that the influence of Slavery upon productive energy is like the blight of mildew—that it is a moral and a social evil; that it does violence to the rights of man, as a thinking, reasoning, and responsible being; that its existence in this territory will shut out free labor, because the free man will not submit himself to the degradation which attaches to labor wherever Slavery exists. Influenced by such considerations, the free States will oppose the introduction of Slavery into the territory which may be acquired."

In speaking of the *right* of slaveholders to hold their slaves in the Territories of the United States, he further said:

"On the other hand, the slave States claim that this territory will be acquired, if acquired at all, by the blood and treasure of all the States of the Union, to become the joint property of all; to be held for the benefit of all. And they emphatically ask, 'Is it consistent with justice?' His right to acquire and possess property is one of the inherent rights of man, independent of laws and Constitutions. Not so with the right to his slave; that is AN UNNATURAL, AN ARTIFICIAL, A STATUTE RIGHT; and when he voluntarily passes with a slave to a Territory, where the statute recognising the right does not exist, then at once the right ceases to exist. THE SLAVE BECOMES A FREE MAN, WITH JUST AS MUCH RIGHT TO CLAIM THE MASTER, AS THE MASTER TO CLAIM THE SLAVE."

This is precisely where the Republican party now stand. And who is Governor Dana? Now Minister to Bolivia, *and appointed by President Pierce.*

The Legislature responded, and passed the following resolutions, with only six nays in the House, and by a large majority in the Senate:

"*Resolved*, That the sentiment of this State is profound, sincere, and almost universal, that the influence of Slavery upon productive energy is like the blight of mildew; that it is a moral and social evil; that it does violence to the rights of man, as a thinking, reasonable, and responsible being. Influenced by such considerations, this State will oppose the introduction of Slavery into any territory which may be acquired as an indemnity for claims upon Mexico.

"*Resolved*, That, in the acquisition of any free territory, whether by purchase or otherwise, we deem it the duty of the General Government to extend over the same the Ordinance of seventeen hundred and eighty-seven, with all its rights and privileges, conditions and immunities.

"*Resolved*, That our Senators be instructed, and our Representatives requested, to support and carry out the principles of the foregoing resolutions."

August 2, 1848, the Legislature of Maine, still strongly Democratic, passed the following resolutions relating to the extension of Slavery in newly-acquired territory:

"*Resolved*, That Maine duly appreciates the concession and compromises which led to the adoption and establishment of the Constitution of the United States; and she will cheerfully and honestly abide by the letter and spirit of them. At the same time she will firmly resist all demands for their enlargement and extension.

"*Resolved*, That the sentiment of this State is profound, sincere, and almost universal, that the influence of Slavery upon productive energy is like the blight of mildew; that it is debasing and degrading in its influence upon free labor; that it is a moral and social evil; that it does violence to the rights of man as a rational, thinking, and accountable being; influenced by these and other important considerations, this State will firmly oppose the introduction of Slavery into any territory acquired as an indemnity for claims upon Mexico.

"*Resolved*, That it is the duty of Congress to prevent, by the exercise of all constitutional power, the extension of Slavery into territory of the United States now free.

"*Resolved*, That our Senators in Congress are hereby instructed, and our Representatives requested, to support and carry out the principles of the foregoing resolutions."

June 28, 1849, the Democratic party in Maine held a State Convention, at which Hon. John Hubbard was nominated for Governor. This Convention was composed of six hundred delegates, at which the following resolutions were passed—only one solitary member voting against them:

"*Resolved*, That the institution of human Slavery is at variance with the theory of our Government, abhorrent to the common sentiment of mankind, and fraught with danger to all who come within the sphere of its influence; that the Federal Government *possesses adequate power to inhibit its existence in the Territories of the Union; that the constitutionality of this power has been settled by judicial construction, by cotemporaneous expositions, and by repeated acts of legislation;* and that we enjoin upon our Senators and Representatives in Congress to make every exertion, and employ all their influence, to procure the passage of a law *forever excluding Slavery* from the Territories of California and New Mexico.

"*Resolved*, That while we most cheerfully concede to our Southern brethren the right, on all occasions, to speak and act with entire freedom on questions connected with Slavery in the Territories, we claim the exercise of the same right for ourselves; and any attempt, from any quarter, to stigmatize us or our Representatives for advocating or defending the opinions of our people upon this subject, will be repelled as an unwarrantable act of aggression upon the rights of the citizens of this State."

At this Convention a committee, of which Colonel Ephraim K. Smart was Chairman, was raised to report an address to the people, from which address I read the following extract:

"The Whig party of this State will undoubtedly present a candidate in opposition to him, [Hubbard,] who will be a swift advocate of Anti-Slavery principles; but he will, at the same time, necessarily feel himself under greater obligations to give aid and comfort to a President [Taylor] and Cabinet *hostile to the inhibition of Slavery in our Territories.* A Governor with such associates *would utterly fail to exert any moral influence* in favor of FREEDOM IN THE TERRITORIES. The Anti-Slavery professions, we are sure, of one who *is bound to do the bidding of* THE

RESENT CABINET AT WASHINGTON, *will be taken at their true value.* The PEOPLE have become JUSTLY JEALOUS of those *who make such professions*, and at the same time *cling to the great central power at the Capitol, and* FOR FAVOR THERE, *even submit to* THE SACRIFICE OF PRINCIPLES *In the present temper of the times, it will be very difficult for such to obtain power.*"

And who is Colonel Smart? Answer. Collector at Belfast, Maine, *appointed by President Pierce*, while he is now publishing a newspaper called the "*Free Press*," *puffing* the President to the skies, advocating the re-election of General Pierce with a zeal and fanaticism which throws every other Democrat in Maine far into the shade.

Governor Hubbard, after his nomination, was written to by some of his political friends as to his position, and made the following reply:

HALLOWELL, *July* 17, 1849.

GENTLEMEN: Yours of the 16th, requesting a "statement of my views in relation to the *extension* of Slavery into Territories of the United States now free," is before me. The question in all its practical bearings, as a subject of deliberative and solemn legislation, is an extensive one. I can only give here a brief statement of the principles which would guide my action upon it.

First. I believe Congress to have *entire*, constitutional jurisdiction over the whole subject of Slavery in the *Territories* of the United States.

Second. I am opposed to Slavery in all its bearings, moral, social, and political, and especially am I opposed to its *extension.*

Third. I would adopt *all* constitutional and equitable means to prevent the extension of Slavery into Territories now free.

Hoping, gentlemen, that this brief *expose* will meet your views, I am, with sentiments of respect and regard, yours,

JOHN HUBBARD.

Messrs. ADAMS TREAT, THOMAS M. MERROW, WILLIAM MERRIAM, AUTHOR TREAT, JESSE SMART, JOHN HODGDON, P. SIMONTON, G. N. WHITE, NATHAN WORTHING, DANIEL WENTWORTH, JOSEPH BACHELDER, DANIEL SMITH.

In 1854, the Legislature of Maine—being in session at the time the Kansas-Nebraska bill was pending before Congress—passed the following resolutions, but with *six* nays in the House, and only *one* in the Senate:

"*Resolved*, That the Senators in Congress from Maine be instructed, and the Representatives requested, to oppose in every practicable way the passage of the Nebraska bill, so called, so long as it shall contain any provision repealing, abrogating, rescinding, or in any way invalidating, that provision of the act of Congress approved March 6, 1820, commonly called the Missouri Compromise.

"*Resolved*, That the Governor be requested to forward a copy of the above resolution to each of our Senators and Representatives at Washington."

Among those who voted for these resolves were Hon. N. S. Littlefield, a leading Democrat in my State, and four years a member of Congress, and President of the last Democratic State Convention in Maine, held in June last, and Hon. Lot M. Merrill, another leader of the party, who was the Democratic candidate for the United States Senate in opposition to Hon. William P. Fessenden, and is now President of the Senate in Maine.

During the Congressional canvass in my district, in 1854, and a few days before election, my competitor for Congress, Hon. William K. Kimball, came out in a letter, in reply to one addressed to him by Hon. W. H. Vinton and others, inquiring as to his position upon the Slavery question—which letter was extensively circulated through the district—in which Mr. Kimball said:

"Gentlemen, I have received your letter of the 1st instant, and lose no time in replying to it. Upon the general subject of American Slavery, my opinions, perhaps, are not different from your own, or from those usually entertained by Northern men. I regard it as a social, moral, and political evil; and its successful abolition, in my judgment, would be worth almost any price short of the Union itself. The idea of its extension into new Territories must be abhorrent to every right-minded and sound-hearted men. Nothing could induce me to give my vote or influence to establish it on a single foot of free soil."

With this letter in their hands, the friends of Mr. Kimball, on the *very eve of the election*, went through my district, urging men who had formerly been connected with the *Free Soil* party to vote for him, alleging, as a reason, that he was more *ultra* than myself upon the Slavery question, at the same time producing that letter as evidence of that fact.

Mr. Chairman, I could go on at almost any length in proving, by the records of the past, that the Democratic party upon this question have in years past held the same position now occupied by the Republican party; but I have no time to put in much other evidence to this point, which I have collected for this purpose. But I will now return, and desire to propound the same question to the Democratic party, which the Almighty put to Adam after he had sinned, "Where art thou?" and, by the way, that party is very much in the same condition Adam was when thus interrogated; and as he was driven out of Paradise by his Maker for his sins, so the Democratic party has been driven out of power by the *people* for the *same cause*, with now no very good prospect of ever getting back into "Paradise." But to the question and the answer.

After General Cass, in his celebrated "Nicholson letter," in 1848, *wandered off South*, and published to the country the fact that a "change had been going on in his own mind as well as in others," out of respect for, or sympathy with, a great political leader—with a love for the spoils, or an inordinate thirst for power and place, or some *other* reasons, he was soon followed by no inconsiderable number of prominent men of his party. From that day to this, they have been backing down, backing down, and backing down, until the Democratic party has lost every element of nationality, and is now become a mere sectional instrumentality, to *spread Slavery into free territory*, and build a great slave oligarchy to override every other interest in the whole country. To allow Slavery to go into the vast fields of Kansas and Nebraska, the Democratic party united with the South to break down the great banner of Freedom in the repeal of the Missouri Compact. This party is now using its whole power to make Slavery national. Having by sectional legislation exposed every foot of American soil to the withering, blighting mildews of Slavery, the party now hugs the viper to its bosom, and declares eternal hostility to "restoration," or a correction of the great wrong by them committed upon the best interests of the Union.

What is Democracy in 1856? Let us examine this question. In order to a right understanding of this matter, I will call the attention of the Committee to certain resolutions passed by Democratic Conventions in several of the States, as their "platform of principles—as the basis of a national organization."

First, I will read certain resolutions of the Democracy of Alabama, at their late Convention to elect delegates to the Cincinnati Convention. This Convention declared in favor of General Pierce's renomination:

Resolved, "8. That it is expedient that we should be represented in the Democratic National Convention upon *such conditions* as are hereinafter expressed.

"9. That the delegates to the Democratic National Convention, to nominate a President and Vice President, *are hereby expressly instructed to insist* that the said Convention shall adopt *a platform of principles as the basis of a national organization*, prior to the nomination of candidates, unequivocally asserting, in substance, the following propositions: 1. The recognition and approval of the principle of non-intervention by Congress upon the subject of Slavery in the Territories. 2. *That no restriction or prohibition of Slavery in any Territory shall hereafter be made in any act of Congress.* 3. That no State shall be refused admission into the Union because of the existence of Slavery therein. 4. The faithful execution and maintenance of the fugitive slave law.

"10. That if said National Convention shall refuse to adopt the propositions embraced in the preceding resolution, our delegates to said Convention *are hereby positively instructed to withdraw therefrom.*"

The Democratic Convention of Mississippi, which assembled in January last to elect delegates to the same Convention, passed the following resolutions:

Resolved, "4. That our delegates to the next National Convention of the Democratic party, to be held for the purpose of nominating candidates for President and Vice President, are hereby instructed that they are to insist on the adoption by said Convention of a platform of principles which shall contain—

"1. A recognition and adoption of the principles of the act of Congress commonly called the Kansas-Nebraska act.

"2. A pledge to resist all attempts to abolish Slavery in the District of Columbia, or, to prohibit the slave trade between the States.

"3. A pledge to resist all attempts to repeal the fugitive slave bill, or impair its faithful execution."

The Democratic State Convention of *Georgia*, the "Empire State" of the South, which, I think, was holden on the 6th of June last, adopted the following resolutions:

"*Resolved*, That we adopt as our own the following resolution, passed unanimously by the last Legislature of Georgia:

"'*Resolved by the General Assembly of the State of Georgia.* That opposition to the principles of the Nebraska bill, in relation to the subject of Slavery, is regarded by the people of Georgia as hostility to the people of the South, and that all persons who partake in such opposition are unfit to be recognised as component parts of any party or organization not hostile to the South.'

"*Resolved*, That in accordance with the above resolution, whilst we are willing to act in party association with all sound and reliable men in every section of the Union, we are not willing to affiliate with any party that shall not recognise, approve, and carry out, the principles and provisions of the Nebraska-Kansas act; and that the Democratic party of Georgia will cut off all party connection with every man and party at the North or elsewhere that does not come up fully and fairly to this line of action."

I have no time to refer to resolutions of Democratic Conventions in other States; they are all of the same tenor.

The Democratic platform has three principal planks:

1. The Constitution of the United States carries Slavery into the Territories, and there protects it;

2. No restriction or prohibition of Slavery in the Territories; and

3. The maintenance and execution of the fugitive slave law.

Here is a platform constructed exclusively to favor Southern interests. Is it a national benefit to extend Slavery into the Territories, or is it done for the benefit of a section? Was not the fugitive slave law made for the benefit of the *South*, and do not its supporters demand its execution to protect *Southern* interests?

The Democratic platform is *sectional* in all its parts; and to call it a "national" platform is a libel upon the common sense of every man who reads it.

With all these facts glaring them in the face, the members of the so-called Democratic party, the supporters of the present national Administration, have the unblushing impudence to stand up, and say to those of us who have, on the stump and at the ballot-box, through good report and evil report, supported Jackson, and Van Buren, and Polk, and Pierce, (until he forsook his friends and abandoned his platform,) and have clung to the Democratic party like the mariner to the wreck, until there was not a single plank of its good old platform left to save us from perdition, that we have left the Democratic party—that we have changed and gone over to Abolitionism—when they know, and we know, and the whole world knows, that they are the men that have changed, *they* are the deserters, that they have gone off and offered sacrifices to strange gods, while we are defending the sacramental altars and consecrated fires of the "God of our fathers." While we are, in good faith, maintaining and defending the doctrine of Jefferson and the Democratic party, they are bowing down and worshiping the Dagon god of African Slavery.

But it may be said the Cincinnati Convention will not adopt the platform dictated by the several State Convention I have referred to. If any one entertains this opinion, he is grossly mistaken. What says the Democracy of Alabama? They instruct their delegates to "withdraw," unless the Convention comes up to the mark; while the Democrats of Georgia declare they "will cut off all party connection with *every man and party at the North*, or *elsewhere*, that does not fully and fairly come up to this line of action." It may be a bitter dose for Northern Democrats, and they may at first resist it; but it will be of no use, for they will have to drink the poisoned draught to the very dregs. Yes, gentlemen, you have got to take the whole dose; and, however bitter and nauseating it may be, you have not only got to swallow it, but say you love it. Every Northern Democrat will have to mount the Juggernaut car of Slavery, "hold the reins, or crack the whip," or be thrown overboard to be crushed under the ponderous weight of its gigantic wheels. An honorable gentleman from South Carolina [Mr. KEITT] the other day, in eloquent but plain language, announced to the Democratic party the line of policy it had got to pursue to receive Southern support. That gentleman said:

"The Democratic party at the North has been cut down in the fight. It has passed through fire and water. It has come out cleansed, with whitened garments. It is now strong enough to do battle for the Constitution. Will you swell it, for the spoils, with a motley horde, wearing soiled and tattered robes? If you will, *give the platform to the South*, and the *man* to the North." * * * * *

"The South should establish in the platform the principle, that the right of a Southern man to his slave is *equal* in its length and breadth to the right of the Northern man to his horse. She should make the recognition of the right full, complete, and indisputable."

There is one other piece of evidence I will offer upon this point. Franklin Pierce and his Administration are endorsed by the Democratic party. Of course, what he believes they believe. Now, to show his position and that of the party who support him, I will read an extract of a letter from Senator Evans, of South Carolina, recently written and published, recommending his State to go into the Cincinnati Convention. He says:

"President Pierce is a man after our own heart. Both in words and deeds he comes nearer to our opinions than any man who has preceded him for the last thirty years. Our vote may give him the nomination, and my best judgment is that we ought to join in the selection."

In the face of these facts, we hear it proclaimed in these Halls, upon the stump, and everywhere, that the Democratic party is a *national* party. Members of this Southern-sectional party talk with great flippancy about "national Democrats," "national Democracy;" and almost in the same breath denounce the only truly national party in the country as "Black Republicans," sectionalists, and fanatics. Black Republicans! Who can help admiring the taste of a party who, for the want of argument to sustain their cause, resort to the doubtful experiment of dealing in opprobrious epithets? "Black Republicans!" Sir, let the party whose very existence is shrouded by the "black" pall of Egyptian night, first wash out the "black" stains of its own pollution, before it deals out contemptuous, reproachful terms upon its neighbors.

Mr. Chairman, before closing my remarks, I desire to notice another charge of a more serious character, brought against the Republican party. The members of this party are charged with being "disunionists." Never was there a charge more unfounded, more untrue. I call upon gentlemen who make this groundless assumption to bring out your *proof*, or "back out." But it was said on this floor, prior to the organization of this House, that the distinguished gentleman from Massachusetts, who with so much ability and impartiality presides over our legislative deliberations, upon a certain occasion said, there "*might* come a contingency when he should be willing to let the Union slide;" and almost any amount of holy horror was expressed by the Administration members of the House over this rumor.

Now, sir, supposing the honorable Speaker did make this remark—which I do not admit—it is no threat of disunion; it expresses no desire for disunion; and it never can be tortured into the expression of a sentiment *favorable* to the dissolution of the Union under any contingency. I defy any gentleman to point me to a single Republican Convention, in any part of the country, that has ever been holden, where anything like disunion sentiments have been uttered. These charges of disunion against the Republican party, or any of its members, when investigated and weighed in the balance of truth, will all disappear, like the "baseless fabric of a vision." Neither is there anything in the political opinions or platform of the Republican party, that *tends* to a disruption of these States. We revere the Constitution, and live up to all its obligations; and when we are charged with disloyalty to this great charter of Freedom, we hurl back the charge, and deny the impeachment.

But who makes these charges against the Republican party? What political organization stands up to charge the Republicans of this country with political treason? It is the so-called Democratic party that has done it, and is now doing it. Sir, this issue has been forced upon us, and we accept it. We will not only act on the defensive, but we "carry the war into Africa." How stands the Nebraska Democracy upon this question?

I have some recollection about a Southern Convention at Nashville, in June, 1850. I do not say for what purpose this meeting was called. I will let Colonel Trotti, a delegate from South Carolina to said Convention, give his understanding of the matter, by giving an extract of a speech made by him at the meeting at which he was chosen. It may be found in the *National Intelligencer*, in June, 1850. He says, in giving his own views:

"That Convention should say to the non-slaveholding States, the South will maintain her rights and equality in the Union, *or she will dissolve it.*"

In this Convention figured several distinguished gentlemen of the Democratic party. One of the resolutions there adopted declares

"That the slaveholding States *cannot* and WILL NOT submit to the enactment by Congress of any law imposing onerous conditions and restraints upon the rights of masters to remove with their property into the Territories of the United States."

I think a majority of the meeting, after getting together, were opposed to taking any *violent* measures to bring about a rupture with the General Government; yet Governor Foote, of Mississippi, in a speech in the United States Senate, July 18, 1850, says:

"That there were disunionists there, (though I regret to acknowledge it,) is *a fact which cannot be denied*, for several gentlemen who acted a prominent part in the Convention are understood to have unfurled the flag of disunion since the Convention adjourned."—*Appen. Cong. Globe, vol.* 22, *p.* 1320.

Hon. Jefferson Davis, now Secretary of War, in a speech in the United States Senate, June 27, 1850, when speaking of "disunion," said:

"It is an alternative not to be anticipated—one to which I could look forward to as the last resort; but it is one, let me say, which *under certain contingencies I am willing to meet;* and I leave my constituents to judge when that contingency arrives."—*Cong. Globe.*

I could go on and read from speeches of eminent gentlemen of the Democratic party, in times past, in which they make direct threats to dissolve the Union; but I will only read two or three extracts from speeches made by Democrats upon this floor, containing their opinions upon this question.

An honorable member from South Carolina, [Mr. Brooks,] in a debate in this House on the 24th of December last, said:

"The gentleman from Massachusetts has announced to the world that, in certain contingencies, he is willing to let the Union slide. Now, sir, let his contingencies be reversed, and I am willing to let the Union slide; ay, sir, to *aid in making it slide.*"

Another honorable member from Virginia, [Mr. McMULLIN,] in a debate in this House on the 20th of December last, said:

"One of the greatest misfortunes of the country, Mr. Clerk, is the fact that our Northern brethren mistake the character of the South. They suppose that the Southern disunionists are confined to the Calhoun wing of the Democratic party. That, sir, is the greatest error that the people of the North have ever fallen into. And I tell you, sir, and I want the country to know it—I want the gentlemen from the free States, our Republicans, our Seward Republicans, our Abolitionists, or whatever else you may be called, to know it—that if you restore the Missouri Compromise, or repeal the fugitive slave law, *this Union will be dissolved.*

"If the Government goes into the hands of the North, into the hands of the Republican party, of the Abolition party—for I like to call things by their true names—I say if the Government of the country goes into the hands of the Abolitionists of the North, and they either repeal the fugitive slave law or restore the Missouri Compromise, I tell the House, and I tell the country, that there will then be union at the South upon this question."

The same gentleman goes on still further to say:

"And let me ask gentlemen from the North, if this Union is dissolved, who holds your National Capitol! But let me say to gentlemen of the North, you cannot get possession of this National Capitol.

"The Capitol now belongs to no section. It belongs alike to North, South, East, and West. But, sir, it was erected upon slave territory, and if the hand of disunion shall ever sever the States of this Republic, you shall never take possession of it while I occupy my seat as a Representative upon this floor. And more, I tell them that when the North and the South sever the connection which now binds them together, the North will never take possession of this Capitol unless they pass over my dead body."

The gentleman says this Capitol was erected upon *slave* territory; and, in case of a dissolution, if the North get any part of the public plunder, while he occupies a seat, they will have to "pass over his dead body." When I listened to this remark, it brought "vividly to my recollection a scene that was witnessed in this same slaveholding territory," in August, 1814, when a handful of British soldiers and sailors, after spending about a month upon the waters of the Chesapeake, landed, and dragging their three pieces of artillery up by hand, over this same "slaveholding territory," applied the torch to the Capitol, reduced it to a heap of smouldering ruins, and, after destroying our library and public archives, leisurely re-embarked, and quietly sailed away to other scenes of operation.

The Democratic State Convention of Alabama, before referred to, in their fourth resolution declare—

"That any interference by Congress *for the prevention of Slavery in any of the Territories*, would be an inexcusable and unconstitutional infringement of the rights of the South, which, it is the deliberate sense of this Convention, *it would be the duty of the people of Alabama to resist even to a* DISRUPTION OF THE TIES THAT BIND THIS STATE TO THE UNION."

This is the party which taunts the Republicans with the charge of "disunion." Let this party first "cast the beam out of its own eye," before it undertakes to "cast the mote out of its brother's eye."

Where can you find a Republican Convention passing resolves deliberately threatening to "dissolve the Union," if the particular measures of the party are not adopted, or if the legislation of the country shall not happen to conform to their notions of constitutional law? Sir, we hear a great deal of boasting about "National Democrats"—"National Democracy." These terms mean nothing but this: a party that is in favor of spreading Slavery into free territory. Again, we hear gentlemen declaiming loud and long about our "constitutional obligations," which, when being truly interpreted, mean "catching runaway negroes."

Then, again, we hear the Republican party denounced as *Black* Republicans, *Disunionists*, *Abolitionists.* Very well, we understand why these reproachful terms are applied to the Republicans. It is simply because they believe in the doctrines of the Declaration of Independence, that the Constitution embodies the great principles of personal liberty; it is because they stand upon the old time-honored platform of Washington, of Jefferson, of Franklin, of Langdon, of Madison, and all the early fathers. Sir, could the Father of his Country awake from the tomb, and leave the quiet retreats of his own Mount Vernon, and his stately form again revisit the national Capitol bearing his name—could the sainted spirit of the immortal Jefferson be reunited to the dust that now reposes amid the solitudes of Monticello, and again mingle with the living, they would both be denounced by this same Democratic party with contumelious opprobriums; they would both be denounced as Black Republicans, Abolitionists, traitors to this great Republic, which their wisdom and patriotism founded.

Mr. Chairman, we are gravely told, in this House and other places, that if the Democratic party are defeated in the next Presidential election, and the Republican party elect their candidate to the Presidential chair, *the Union will be dissolved.* Let me say to gentlemen on the other side of the House, not tauntingly, but respectfully, in the face of your threat, we shall beat you if we can. If we succeed, (as I trust in God we shall,) then I say again, not to menace, but to warn you, *Dissolve this glorious Union if you dare do it.* You have practiced this same game too long—you have "dissolved the Union" *too many times* before, to disturb the repose or unsettle the nerves of the intelligent, patriotic citizens of these thirty-one States. Gentlemen, "Othello's occupation's gone." Your thundering gasconade, that the "Union will be dissolved," has died away in harmless accents, and ceases to alarm even the fearful and timid. But, if gentlemen really desire to dissolve the Union, why not *do* something besides talk and threaten? Why not begin—why not try the fearful experiment? You need not wait a day on the account of the Republican party. We are as willing to meet you *now* as at any future time, and settle this question, if you want to try it. Yes, gentlemen, we will meet you upon this question whenever and wherever you present it. The Republicans of these United States, upon this issue, have but one flag, the "stars and stripes." Not one star upon its floating folds will they ever see bedimmed or blotted out—not one stripe disfigured by the lawless hand of treason. They have but one motto—the motto transmitted to the American people by the immortal Jackson, "The Union—it must be preserved;" and, like the old hero of the Hermitage, they are, every man of them, ready to "swear by the Eternal" it shall never perish at the hands of any party, North or South.

A friend some weeks since placed in my hands a pamphlet, containing the speeches by the distinguished Senator from California, Mr. Weller, and of three distinguished gentlemen belonging to this House—Colonel Orr of South Carolina, ex-Speaker Cobb of Georgia, and General Lane of Oregon—made in Concord, New Hampshire, prior to the last election in that State. Colonel Orr near his closing remarks is reported to have said:

"Roll back this swelling tide of Republicanism. If you desire to save the Union, you must overwhelm it."

This sounds very much like Caleb Cushing's 'crushing out." The distinguished gentleman calls upon his political friends to "overwhelm Republicanism." Yes, gentlemen, if you "desire to save the Union, you must overwhelm it." But how did the descendants of "Molly Stark," the unterrified yeomanry of the glorious old Granite State, respond to this call. Who was 'overwhelmed" in New Hampshire? Was it the "swelling tide of Republicanism?" No, sir! No, sir! It was "sectional Democracy"—the legions of the forlorn hope of all that remains of that once honored and respectable party, led on by General Pierce—that was "overwhelmed." The honest people of that patriotic State "overwhelmed" them, buried them up, and with the funereal rites perished the last fading hopes of Franklin Pierce of a re-election to the Presidency Who was "overwhelmed" in Rhode Island a few weeks since, and who in Connecticut a few days since? Was it the "swelling tide of Republicanism?" No, sir; it was this same "sectional Democracy"—a party that has gone so far South, that it has even lost sight of the "North star."

But, again, the Republicans are denounced as "agitators! agitators!!" Sir, who *began* this agitation? The very party who now denounce it. Yes, gentlemen Democrats, you fired "the fagot pile," and now, when its roaring flames send their ghastly, lurid glare in every direction all over the whole Union, you turn round and denounce your innocent neighbor with incendiarism, when you yourselves applied the smoking torch. *You* have raised the wind, now you must "ride the whirlwind."

But what party *continues* agitation upon the Slavery question? Who sends message after message into both Houses of Congress, falsifying the great truths of history—denouncing the people of the free States, falsely charging them with numerous derelictions of duty? Who sends Governors to Kansas to enforce the brutal laws of a bogus Legislature upon the squatter sovereigns of that Territory? What party is now moving heaven and earth to force Slavery into Kansas, against the will of the people of that devoted Territory, and in direct violation of an old compact, to which both sections of the Union were a party? I leave the people and the country to answer these questions.

Mr. Chairman, we are deliberately told by the Administration party, that if the Missouri Compromise is restored, and Kansas made free—that if the old compact of 1820 is substantially carried out—it "will be an end of the Union." You make the issue, gentlemen—we accept it. It is a part of the mission of the Republican party to make Kansas a free State; and gentlemen on the other side of the House have chosen Kansas as the great battle-ground of Freedom, and there we meet you. The designs and purposes of the Republican party upon this vital question are like the "laws of the Medes and Persians," unalterable. Our Southern brethren, more than thirty years ago, for a consideration paid in hand, solemnly agreed that the vast and fertile regions of Kansas and Nebraska should forever be *free* territory; and we mean to hold you to the contract.

The great Republican party has taken its position. Its banner has been unfurled, and now proudly floats in the breezes of heaven, while upon its folds are inscribed in golden capitals of living light—NO MORE EXTENSION OF THE FOOT-PRINTS OF SLAVERY [illegible] TERRITORY. Around this banner are r[illegible] the patriotic from all sections in the Union. [illegible]

But one spirit animates the great army of Freedom. Their watchword is "*Onward! onward!*" their battle cry, the soul-stirring words of the immortal Henry—"Give me liberty, or give me death."

WASHINGTON, D. C.
BUELL & BLANCHARD, PRINTERS.
1856.

TO THE OPPONENTS OF SLAVERY-EXTENSION.

The Publishing Association of Washington intend to stereotyp the Speeches delivered in Congress during the present session, an other Documents, suitable for use in the coming Presidential Cam paign. In order to facilitate their circulation as much as possible the Association will furnish and mail them, singly, to such name and post offices as may be desired, at one dollar per hundred for doc uments of eight pages, and two dollars per hundred for document of sixteen pages, free of postage. For packages of one hundred, c more, sent at the cost of purchasers, documents of eight pages, sixty two cents, and documents of sixteen pages, one dollar and twenty five cents.

Persons sending us ten dollars and upwards can have the amoun placed to their credit, and copies of each Speech or Document issue by the Association during the Campaign will be sent to their addres or to such names as they may direct, in such quantities as may be de sired, until the money sent is exhausted. Address

LEWIS CLEPHANE, *Secretary*,
Washington, D. C.

BUELL & BLANCHARD, Printers, Washington, D. C.

www.ingramcontent.com/pod-product-compliance
Lightning Source LLC
LaVergne TN
LVHW020639110826
845149LV00004B/1293